D1233171

Published by Creative Education
P.O. Box 227, Mankato, Minnesota 56002
Creative Education is an imprint of
The Creative Company
www.thecreativecompany.us

Design by The Design Lab
Production by Chelsey Luther
Art direction by Rita Marshall
Printed in the United States of America

Photographs by Dreamstime (Steve Byland, Mirceax),
Getty Images (Danita Delimont, Steve & Dave
Maslowski), iStockphoto (Steve Byland, Ronald
Glovan, kumakuma1216), Shutterstock (Charles
Brutlag, FloridaStock, IbajaUsap, Martha Marks),
SuperStock (Minden Pictures, James Urbach)

Library of Congress Cataloging-in-Publication Data
Riggs, Kate.
Woodpeckers / Kate Riggs.
p. cm. — (Amazing animals)
Summary: A basic exploration of the appearance,
behavior, and habitat of woodpeckers, nature's drum-
mers. Also included is a story from folklore explaining
how woodpeckers take good care of their young.
Includes bibliographical references and index.
ISBN 978-1-60818-352-4
1. Woodpeckers—Juvenile literature. I. Title. II.
Series: Amazing animals.

QL696.P56R54 2014
598.7'2—dc23   2013005401

First Edition
9 8 7 6 5 4 3 2 1

WOODPECKERS

BY KATE RIGGS

CREATIVE EDUCATION

Acorn woodpeckers live in the American West and Mexico

Woodpeckers are birds that peck holes in trees. There are about 180 kinds of woodpeckers in the world today. They live in woods and forests on five of Earth's **continents**.

continents Earth's seven big pieces of land

Woodpeckers

usually have black, white, gray, or brown feathers. Some have red, orange, or yellow markings, too. Woodpeckers have short legs and long tail feathers. They use their tail feathers to balance when they are pecking wood.

Red-bellied woodpeckers have black-and-white feathers on their backs

Some of the smallest woodpeckers in the world are the pygmy (*PIG-mee*) woodpeckers that live in Asia. They are only five inches (12.7 cm) long. The largest woodpeckers can be about 20 inches (51 cm) long.

Pileated woodpeckers (opposite) are about the size of a crow

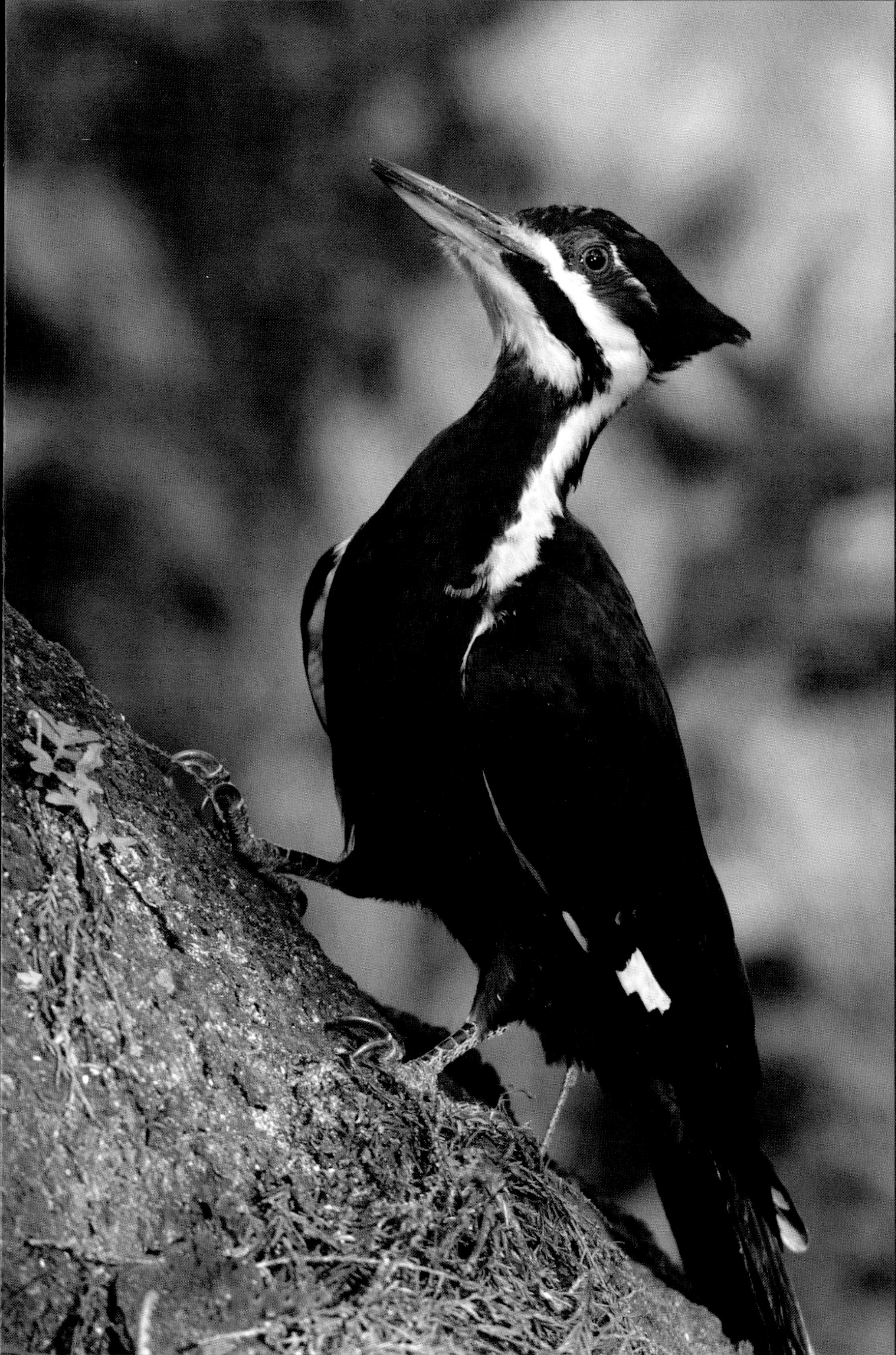

Woodpeckers

are named for what they do: they peck wood to get to food. Woodpeckers use their beaks to drill holes. A woodpecker can tap against wood up to 28 times per second. The birds have strong necks that do not get tired.

Woodpeckers drill big holes to make a place for a nest

Woodpeckers feed baby insects called larvae to their young

Woodpeckers eat insects, nuts, sap, and other foods. Ants are a woodpecker's favorite insect food. Woodpeckers that live in hot, dry lands called deserts eat fruit from the cactus.

cactus a thick plant that has sharp spines instead of leaves

sap a sugary liquid found in trees

Northern flickers have six to eight young at a time

A mother lays eggs in a nest. The mother and father keep the eggs warm. Then the baby woodpeckers **hatch**. A baby woodpecker does not have any feathers. Its feathers come in after about a week. The parents bring food to the baby birds.

hatch come out of an egg

Woodpeckers that do not have babies live alone. Male and female woodpeckers call to each other by making drumming sounds. A woodpecker can live 4 to 11 years in the wild.

Female (top) and male acorn woodpeckers can be told apart by their coloration

Woodpeckers drum and peck on wood. They fly from tree to tree. Sometimes they peck on posts and even houses! Woodpeckers that eat nuts store them in the summer. Then they eat the nuts in the winter.

A tree that holds a woodpecker's nuts is called a granary

Woodpeckers live in many places near people. People can hear them drumming and drilling. It is fun to see and listen to these noisy birds!

Woodpeckers make a mess when they drill into trees

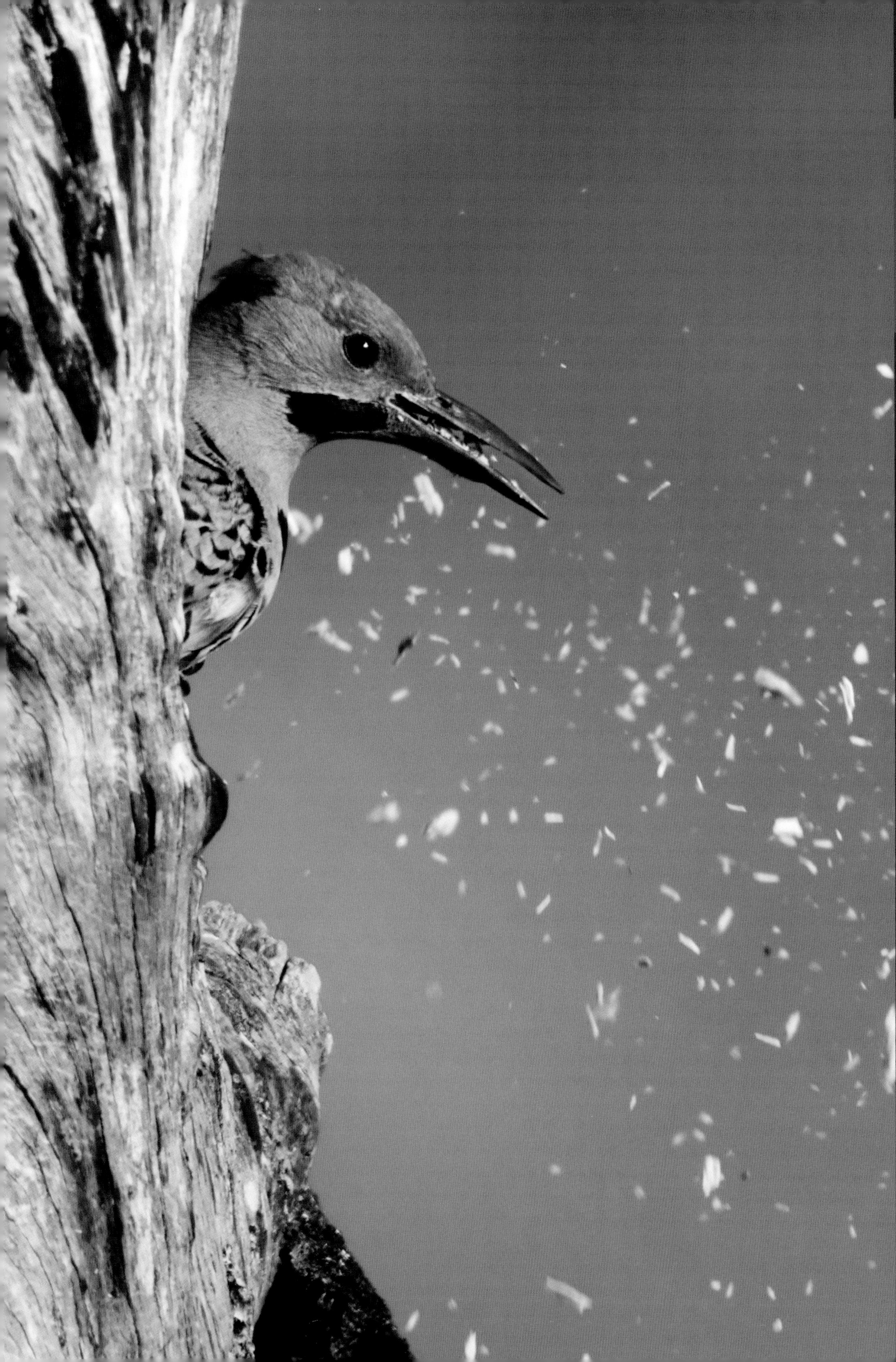

A Woodpecker Story

Are woodpeckers good parents? People in North America told a story about this. They said that the turkey and the woodpecker had a contest to see who was the better mother. The turkey had so many babies that she could not keep track of them all. Many of them died. But the woodpecker kept her young safe inside a tree. So the woodpecker was put in charge of watching over people.

Read More

Mania, Cathy. *Woodpecker in the Backyard*. New York: Franklin Watts, 2000.

Schuetz, Kari. *Woodpeckers*. Minneapolis: Bellwether Media, 2012.

Websites

DLTK's Woodpecker Craft
http://www.dltk-kids.com/animals/mwoodpecker.html
Learn how to make your own woodpecker out of a toilet paper roll!

National Geographic Video: Acorn Stash
http://video.nationalgeographic.com/video/kids/animals-pets-kids/wild-detectives-kids/wd-ep6-hidingacorns/
Watch this video to see how woodpeckers store food for the winter.

Index